BERTHA & OTHER PLAYS

BERTHA & OTHER PLAYS

by

Kenneth Koch

GROVE PRESS, INC., NEW YORK

Library of Congress Catalog Card Number: 66-14108

First Printing

A number of these plays were previously published: *Pericles* in *Poems*, DeNagy, New York, 1953; *Bertha* in *Evergreen Review*; *Six Improvisational Plays* and *The Building of Florence* in *Art and Literature*; scenes from *Angelica* in *Poetry* and *Portfolio & Art News Annual*; *Guinevere* in *Yugen*, copyright © 1961 by Le Roi Jones and Hettie Cohen; *The Building of Florence*, *The Return of Yellowmay* and *The Revolt of the Giant Animals* in *C*.

Manufactured in the United States of America

For Katherine Koch

NOTE

These plays are in chronological order except for the scenes from *Angelica*. *Angelica* was written as an opera libretto for a composer in 1958, but the project never reached completion. A text of the whole libretto exists, but I don't think it is the final version of the work. A note on the plot accompanies the scenes included here.

—K.K.

CONTENTS

PERICLES

Scene 1

FRIEND:

I stop and go, Pericles.

PERICLES:

Because we have come to find this land

FRIEND:

In the midst of truth,
climates, guitars

PERICLES:

This breeze is smaller than my mouth.

FRIEND:

O Pericles
what is a leader?

PERICLES:

How we have grown, dears, since we've
been from Greece!

9

FRIEND:
How tall a music

PERICLES:
Lies wasting on the shore.

Scene 2

ANOTHER MAN:
Here I sit.

Scene 3

A WOMAN:
Not that the gnat of smallness itself
has anything to offer the beach
with and through, without our tears
as if some tea had raised a blind
into the concussion of nonsense,
and a coughing death.

In Athens I saw twenty-nine old people
and the sidewalk was faery.
Oh everywhere the rats struck down ribbons,
heaven. A slave-ship hides my ears.

O friends
amid the fornication of signposts
I saw a new Greece
arise!

Scene 4

FRIEND:

> You know. And yet
> he is bothered by the misery of pebbles
> which hat the lovely show
> in which he dies and does appear.
> He: "Take me back to the faucets
> of truth; my mind is a mass."

PERICLES:

> Here is freshness and the shore's timeless teeth!

Scene 5

FRIEND:

> There's no midnight mystery
> and no coconuts here to see,
> nothing but the ocean's sea
> which will wash history's tattoos from me;
> I hope to live satisfactorily
> like a capon that's struck by a tree
> and does die gladly
> bereft, O large, of his sexuality.
> Oh as honey fills the bee
> while the waves' orchestra's business spree
> sticks its night in your head like a country,
> and as the madman throws the flea
> to music, helplessly,
> here always shall I be
> and not in idolatry,
> but yet superfluous as a ski

in a barge; while the withered air
reduces baneful boughs to everywhere.

PERICLES:

Goodnight, the parachutes have gone to sleep.

FRIEND:

I stop and go, Pericles.

Scene 6

PERICLES:

The air is Chinese!
I felt so strange
the day after tomorrow.
The stops have been removed
and the bottle is filled with leeks.
In the forest a sparring partner
whispers, "We grow."
O maidenhead of today
O maidenhead of yesterday

FRIEND:

My lord, I found this face in the sand.

PERICLES:

Drop it!

FACE OF ANOTHER MAN:

Help!

Curtain

EPILOGUE

(Spoken by the conductor of the orchestra.)

And would it not have been too late
The gas goes on the gas goes off
And we stood there with pure roots
In silence in violence one two one two
Will you please go through that again
The organ's orgasm and the aspirin tablet's speechless
    spasm.

THE MERRY STONES

Scene 1

A room in a house by the sea. ROY, *a young man, is lying in bed.* INGELIL, *a young Swedish nurse, is standing at the bedside.*

INGELIL:

Lay down and be slumbering. A cabinet is kind. The music is full of fishes. Have some liberty. Eat colds. Don't be neglected. Board up the hose. Thank the rip tides. Lose collectedness. Break, break the ramps.

ROY:

I went to smiling wrists.

INGELIL:

Govern the deciding wasps. Age new badness. Sign Lohengrin. Be out on the Caspian.

ROY:

Locks were coming in bananas.
Furniture is necks.
Sacrilege is leaning on tiny horse.

A lamprey, oh, has begun to kiss
The sea.

INGELIL:

Use the deigning colors of this cabinet for your win-
dows; only don't, when the winter comes, complain
of the cannon-fare of the horses; for as surely as hay
is tucked into the orphan straw, time will have guess
his last lust in the ephemeral killing bottle. I am a
laziness that comes from a nuttier country; I see to
not understand your flailing indecrepitude. May the
blue star of yesterday pink its liberal summit to that
head, this yours, which, like a revolvement, fats
the walls with lowing circumvention. Oh good-by,
normal!

ROY:

Farewell, moral, and may the neckerchiefs of hum-
ming be kind cousins to your gloom. The illiterate
flowers are incompatible with shows.

Scene 2

A room. JIM, *a young man, is lying in bed.*

JIM:

If I should die, myself,
Give me the wallpaper
And wrap me up around the ceiling,
As if sky to an ornament.
Oh how fitting is my known
Beneath the dense whack of the sheet;
If mattress-covers in truth
Were known, ah, steel would be riven!

But I am back to my back
On flowers, like the Chinese river
Sink-you-and-go-long-go-she-go,
And music is everywhere.
I wonder if this knife
Would not slay me like an imbecile
If I let it fall, down snow-light
In registered rocks from here—

(*He seems to stab himself.*)

Oh, lie steep as a swan!
Exaggeration of comments, then help me!

Scene 3

A bare stage.

MASTER OF CEREMONIES (*about forty-five years old*):
Here are the starriest chain-weaving starvers
That ever an eyeball sees, O chasing frankness with
sleds!

(*Exit* M.C.)

FIRST SHOW-GIRL:
I am the music bell of doughnuts, ruthful ball,
Beds at night in the Sierras, the beach of brass
That an annoyedly soft breast dims,
And my revealing counsels are foolish with sonnets.

SECOND SHOW-GIRL:
The least of time's molluscs, and last of the golden
hinters
Am I, come down to Seventieth with my scants on!

I am teas
Without formulas! London!

THIRD SHOW-GIRL:

I am the bashful banditress of beans,
Irritants, coca-cola, and steaks.
I lie beyond the built-in Sierra of plates
To see our cares mated to a roach in oblivion!

MASTER OF CEREMONIES (*re-enters; he is much younger*):

So seize your hats,
Be merry as a phone,
And cry out at the graying night,
"Oh thou high pajama of happiness!"
Last week
I felt it know you care so cold.

Scene 4

In the Sierras.

ELDERLY MAN:

A season is my birthright; for which reason
Winter is very indebted to hats. We are
Condemning you to
Breath under water.

BOB:

But I am a mountain lad! my whole bearing and being
Calls out for freedom from Fordham.

ELDERLY MAN:

Nevertheless, go under;

And when you rise, the flowers of heat
Will open your eyes,
And you shall see this Sierra
As the beautiful door to the bust
Of the highly chlorinate female wind
Who hides the masculine hills in her boxes;
The magic of forceful steam
Will be yours, and the shying parts of airplanes,
The linked romance of degustation
And paralysis, to lie on, in the nights of tragic green.

BOB:

I am asea with lust!

ELDERLY MAN:

Yet no more forgotten
Than a cast-iron ring.
We are bored by the mid-day of flowers,
The Romeo riling amid the wildflowers,
And the beggar the boar smiling into the flowers.

Scene 5

A hotel room.

AL (*a young husband*):

There is another scene than this hotel room!
Where the boy tries to take his life!
O monsters, my wife!

NELLIE (*his wife*):

He is walking the floor in rings!

AL:

I once saw a Swedish stand amid the flowers, and throw blood upon dancers, while sick man, roving up on the bourgeoisie, held in his hats the swan of their hands, as though a telephone rings.

(*Ring. It is a doorbell. Enter* BOB.)

NELLIE (*throws her arms around* AL):
Did you send for the bugles of Lancaster?

Curtain

WITHOUT KINSHIP

Scene 1

Somewhere on the lawn of Longfellow's House, in Cambridge, Massachusetts. A nightingale leans over her ironing board.

NIGHTINGALE:
It is small and white.

IRONING BOARD:
Over the pill and far away
I hot a vision of white
So mental, that where carpets kneel.

NIGHTINGALE:
Loon, pyramid, shine-shine,
O bark that has suds' little keel
In the gemlight, O bibarkcycle—

IRONING BOARD:
Am I then, lady's head,
Which you have tied unto a knot?

PEBBLE:

Kenneth stands for constancy,
Roommate for regret;
Our Christian society for clemency
To the dancing Sundays of seas' frenetic egret.
Janice stands for Japanese
Mapletrees, which stream about this yard
As though a mariner'd come here
To find his ocean hard.

GIRL PEBBLE:

O Melvin!

PEBBLE:

Charmian!

(*They go together and form a driveway.*)

Scene 2

The Nurse.

NURSE:

These modern gems have laziness;
My hat is his. This Denver sun
Shines on and down
What grassy slopes?
Season! here is the soap factory;
There is the charged balloon.
My grandfather at eighty offered
The stanza a million dollars
That could make him feel as though
He were really a lagoon.

His face is now seldom
More than unscientific explanation
For a rug. Oh, carry me, impossible slug!

(*She lies down too and becomes driveway.*)

Scene 3

Roadway, driveway. PATIENCE *and* HANDY *are in their car.*

HANDY:

Harrisonville to Spokane
In nine thousand three hundred and sixty-seven
Days, it doesn't seem impossible!

PATIENCE:

A storm moderates me this end.

NIGHTINGALE (*from below, as she and her ironing board
are now part of the driveway*):
Gazing with hope

PEBBLE:

This morning upon the

NURSE:

Foolish capers in the sun

GIRL PEBBLE:

I understood for the last time

IRONING BOARD:

How the fanshaped crisscrosses,
Which speak to everything, are done.

FOOTBALL (*comes flying through*):
> I gave, for love, my terrifying heart.
> Ah, that laughing, papery summer, when we kissed
> The leaves of every down, that showed the field
> A prayer, and at evening a park.

HANDY:
> Please, Patience, take this green dress!

PATIENCE:
> O branches! where is the collie of happiness?

EVERYONE:
> Woof! Woof!

Curtain

EPILOGUE

GIRL:
> If you can fail to understand
> I have been formed to represent where
> Canada actually begins to understand
> Herself as a country and where carfare is the red
>> postage stamps
> For freedom. When the oranges come in to stand
> For a cafeteria, I will be here to kiss you then.

End

GUINEVERE
or *The Death of the Kangaroo*

Scene: a street, a plaza.

GUINEVERE:
Oh solids!

GIRAFFE (*moving along the sidewalk*):
Yes, and you know, last evening there were junctures
of drunken breath's dear pink flowers on my lariat.
He put around me. They said, "Denmark and the
vitrines! nameless one!"

WEISSER ELEFANT (*crossing the street toward the* GIRAFFE
at right angles):
I remember.

GUINEVERE (*sings*):
With soles on her shoes,
She takes the gyroscope
Between her fingers,
And, quietly, it spins.

KANGAROO (*waiting at point where the paths of
the* GIRAFFE *and* WEISSER ELEFANT *cross*):
The. O the the. The. I gave the pillow a cussing
sandwich. America said, "A tree." The manager lay
dead. Cuff links.

GIRAFFE (*pausing*):
Listen, darlings, don't be so sassy. Do you remember
when Chicago was only fingertips?

ALL (*sing*):
Though circumstances may collect our iced man!

MAN (*who enters*):
Unpin these benches that you may descry
The leafs beneath them. Lovers know my voice
As that which is or was most at the docks
Before they stopped shipping roses to say "vivre,"
O macadam. A child sicklier than restaurant
Waits for the marrying blue of a stiff morning.
We seem to go to run about in a stiff roustabout,
Cuter is the pear of string. Common last touch
Is to die at the nest. Roommate, charm bracelet,
Oh I swear, this is Mexico City.

CHIEFTAIN:
He is falling toward me like the charm bracelet
I saw laughing out of the window. At this minute a
    giraffe
Knows the cow who is offering night my atlas.
The wind, curving from Chinese charm bracelet
To charm bracelet, seems to counsel me, "Dollars,
Feenamint, dollars, gunsmoke." After one night
With Dolores, I visited the Huguenot people.

CAPTAIN:

Anchors aweigh!

> (*The plaza with all its occupants floats
> away;* VENUS *rises from the waves.*)

VENUS:

Listen. Listen to the bouquet.
Baby, that placing powder in the pistols,
Married, and placing pistols in the bouquet,
Left me to be long ago at this moment,
Lively, the goddess, a headache. A market
Of fleas!

> (*It is Paris, a Place.* VENUS *disappears.*)

FIRST FLEA:

Let go of my left elbow.

SECOND FLEA:

That's your pot belly!

A PINK GIRL:

I chanced to find these two
Arguing. There were sadly smoke,
Giant cow-guns, shoguns; and, it appears,
A glass page blonder as a neck of blue jeers.

GIRAFFE & VENUS (*entering together*):

Aren't we a stray couple
From No Land? Oh when
Will catching diseases fly in our plane?

PILOT:

Never! Take everyone a box.

(*He passes out little boxes, which, when they are opened, reveal white pieces of paper.*)

WEISSER ELEFANT (*reads*):
"The bench you are sitting on is made of orange boa constrictors which have been treated with piratical chocolate Georgia-bannisters. The Maryland of your face. Despite what you have been, ho ho, the incinerator is not a call-girl. Depart before the ice cream melts." Mine is about food!

GUINEVERE (*throwing herself on* WEISSER ELEFANT):
O my lover, my lover!

PILOT:
Wait a minute. Read yours.

GUINEVERE (*gazes into* VENUS's *face*):
"Your head may be paralyzed by lint." Orchids! buzz saws!

ORCHIDS:
This is not blood. This is an orchard.
Through which you may walk. Like a bug.

BUZZ SAW:
Everybody: one, two, three!
Plywood!
Goldsmith!
Sun glasses!

(*The plaza splits in two like an orange.* WEISSER ELEFANT *eats one half of it. On the other half,* GUINEVERE *is playing a guitar to the* KANGAROO, *and playing cards are falling from his pocket. In the slight breeze one can just make out the chorus of neckties. It seems as if the Old World had become the New. A* MOUSE *enjoys this séance.*)

MOUSE:

God plays the guitar
And Religion listens.
The weary squash
Lurks beside the lotus.
See! the glass buildings
Decide nothing.
We are the sobbing world,
Just as they are in the nude.

GUINEVERE (*very loud*):
Photomatic bad living
Gigantic prisms. Beaued. Gee. Leaves!

KANGAROO (*softly*):
Pretty Geneva, pretty Southland, beloved orchestra!

GUINEVERE:
I am pink in the nude.

KANGAROO:
Yes yes.

GUINEVERE:
O Joy!

KANGAROO:

    Listen. Baccalaureate. Is that
Prometheus?

MAN (*he is wearing a large mouse head, and plays the guitar*):

    Only the bathroom knees would care
And the table of good red air
Seriously affronts the car
With the yellow daffodils of today.
Somnolent I see an amethyst
Clearing the way for future
Eons, the ragged hoop
And the dippy Fragonard of fluffier days,
Played to the tune of our pablum violin.

GUINEVERE (*throws herself, kissing, against a statue*):

    O you, concede that I am the airport!

MAN WITH MOUSE HEAD:

    America is like an elephant whose baseballs
Are boundaries
Of sunlight. *This* is peppermint,
That billiard shore. Now she gets,
Like horror, the main idea, a stove that is
Brilliant as the curling raspberries and move to his
    heart.
O olives, I know your reputation for fairness,
And every pipe dreams of a shirtwaisted kimono
Beyond the callow limousine of the funnies; but
    Nugent
Drank the coca-cola, and Allen left the boudoir

Where Jane lay thrown like a saint, the music of a
    thumb
Daring the elate, childless strings.
O mothers, weevil, market-place of the Sixties,
What is the road to Gary, China?

GUINEVERE:

Should industry delay,
Or mice parade? Is that a youth group
Signing: "Daft, weird, kind pennons,
Yo-yos and hills, shirts and displays"?

MAN WITH MOUSE HEAD:

O Germany of sofas,
Are we so clear
As beer is harmless?

GIRAFFE:

A shoplifting land of railroad pajamas
Passed my door, evil filmstars.
Huguenot! evil girls of filmstar plantation!

HIPPO:

Yes because we meant to spend the summer;
But now we see the human element
Is merely a white bear, tipping stars
By the briefcase of a violet hand
Meant to inform and believe concatenated
The surface of a wheel-lake, or "morgen"
Meaning "morning" in German. Yes I meant
To thumb a ride along the Champs Elysées,
But the sunny negro
Of handsome stars

Bid for the fingers of my door, and lo! I lay,
The Hippopotamus, sweating as if funny
Water may come true even in the summertime
And—

>   (*Bang! The* HIPPO *falls dead.*)

SOMEONE:

Pure Pins the lobster!

>   (YELLOWMAY *comes in and takes off all
>   Guinevere's clothes;* GUINEVERE *puts her
>   clothes back on.*)

GUINEVERE:

The shortest way to go home yesterday
He always called the best way.
There's no suffering in a limeade
Of clearer captains, carpenters, and shipwrights
From brains solidly
In the pier. O the white shore, the red sea—

>   (YELLOWMAY *takes her hand; they walk
>   along the seashore.*)

YELLOWMAY:

And the works of pineapple.
I have often been a shipmaster
But never a ship. The blow from Tangiers
Never came.

GUINEVERE:

Soldiers waiting at my hammock
Counseled me, "Be as back as soot."
Oh nuts, the chairs have gone away.

YELLOWMAY:

> Paintings of the sea, I won't reveal to you my name is
> Yellowmay.

MAN (*without mouse head*):

> Or the lobster
> That oval
> Which I often noticed.
> I think,
> "Is this a cigar
> Or, baby! maybe
> The license for a white cigarette,
> Given by the shields."
> And when the frog becomes a bicycle,
> Dear days of pineapple,
> Lilac where the giant ripple
> Rushes, as past a kangaroo.

KANGAROO:

> O mournful existence within the matchbox
> With a sullen cockatoo
> Whose brain beats its own division
> And dandy "wawa"—

OCEAN:

> Oh Sweden is endless! the earliest time to drink.

YELLOWMAY:

> Are we drinking in chairs like a column?

GUINEVERE:

> Oh yes, master. Come jinx with the merry columbine!

> > (*Suddenly it is spring. The* HIPPO *appears,*
> > solus, *covered with garlands of flowers.*)

HIPPO:

>Decency of printemps O
>Knocks on my pillow!
>Houses without a door!
>Suitcases which miss my sleeves!
>O bears, you too, on the misty shore
>Of the sea, in whose elbows
>I hear a moth beginning
>To mourn on a blue, beautiful violin.

>>(*The* SKY *descends, covering all with blue;
>>from the empty stage comes a song.*)

VOICE FROM EMPTY STAGE:

>Who cares about them
>In a grouping again
>Or the poking amethyst
>And delicious anthem?
>The bread in the butter box
>And a dictionary—
>The day fears to tell me
>Of white screams. Oh, don't you know it,
>The marriage of blue
>Bells, America, generous, as white screens
>Failing, the magazine basement
>Of archways. Water
>The generous magazines!

>Summery blue daylight,
>The manner of machines,
>Daguerrotype, cigarette store.

>>(*The dead body of the* KANGAROO *is
>>dragged across the stage by a two-horse
>>cart.*)

BERTHA

Scene 1

Oslo, the ramparts.

NOBLE:

The walls of our castles no longer withstand
The barbarian attack!

COUNSELOR:

Seek BERTHA in her haven!

NOBLE:

Bertha! we are at the barbarians' mercy.

BERTHA:

Give the signal for attack!

NOBLE:

Attack? attack? How can we attack?
We are at the barbarians' mercy, they have
surrounded our walls!

BERTHA:

Let me commune with my special gods a little.
Meanwhile, ATTACK!

NOBLE:

BERTHA commands attack!

COUNSELOR:

Oh, the queen is mad!

NOBLE:

Mad, yes—but queen still. Never had Norway fairer
or more brave.

OFFICER:

To the attack, as commanded by Queen Bertha!

OLD MAN:

Unhappy pagans! Soon the wrath of Bertha will be
wreaked on them!

> (BERTHA *appears, clothed in a ring of white
> eagles.*)

BARBARIANS:

Help, help! Back! We are defeated!

> (*They scurry.*)

ALL:

Bertha has saved us from the barbarian menace.

> (BERTHA *retires.*)

Scene 2

A study in the castle.

TEACHER:

> Yes, it's a very interesting tale, that one you tell of
> the battle.
> But why do you think you and your people yourselves
> are not Barbarians?

BERTHA:

> Off with my teacher's head!
>   WHACK!
> Let higher learning be disreinstated!

> (*Banners are sent up all over the kingdom.*)

Scene 3

Bertha's summer lodge.

BERTHA:

> Ah, how sweet it is to take the Norway air
> And breathe it in my own lungs, then out again
> Where it again mingles with the white clouds and
> blue Norwegian sky.
> For I myself, in a sense, am Norway, and when
> Bertha breathes
> The country breathes, and it breathes itself in,
> And so the sky remains perfectly pure Norway.

MESSENGER:
Bertha, the land is at peace.

BERTHA:

Attack Scotland!

Scene 4

A little Scotch frontier town, on the battle lines.

SCOTCHMAN:
They say Queen Bertha's men rage to win all Scotland
as a present for their mad queen.

SECOND SCOTCHMAN:
No one has ever had Scotland defeated for very long;
let Queen Bertha try what she may!

THIRD SCOTCHMAN:
Here come the armies of Bertha, Queen of Norway!

BERTHA (*at the head of her army, in a red and blue uniform; plants a banner*):
Here shall Bertha stay, nor all Scotland conquer!
Just to this flag's wave shall Bertha of Norway's
kingdom reach!
No greed urges the just Norwegian nation to further
spoils.

ALL SCOTCH:
Hurrah for Queen Bertha!

COMMON NORWEGIAN SOLDIER:

She is mad!

(*Trumpets, and dispersal of all troops; the flag alone
remains standing on the snowy stage.*)

Scene 5

The Council Chamber.

COUNSELOR:

Queen Bertha, we are tired of useless wars.

BERTHA:

Useless! Do you call it useless to fight off an invader?

COUNSELOR:

I was not speaking of the Barbarian Wars.

BERTHA:

Well, I was! The council is dismissed.

(*Everyone leaves, including* BERTHA.)

Scene 6

A rose garden.

GIRL:

If Queen Bertha knew we were here!

MAN:

> She'd chop our two heads off, chip chap chop. There's no doubt about it.

GIRL:

> Why does she forbid us young lovers to meet in the garden?

MAN:

> A diseased mind, and the horrid fears of encroaching old age.

> > (*They embrace. Explosion. Both fall dead.*)

BERTHA (*from a castle window*):
> Let there be no more garden meetings.

Scene 7

BERTHA *on her throne.*

BERTHA:

> I am old, I am an old queen. But I still have the power
>   of my childhood
> Contained in my office. If I should lose my office, no
>   more power would accrue
> To my aged and feeble person. But even supposing
>   I keep my power?
> What chance is there that anything really nice will
>   happen to me?

> > (*She plays with a flag, musing.*)

The flag of Norway! Once its colors drove my young
  heart wild
With dreams of conquest, first of the Norwegian flag,
  then of all the other nations in the world . . .
I haven't gotten very far—yet still Bertha is great!
  (*Ringing a bell.*) Call in the High Commissioners!

Scene 8

The Throne Room.

BERTHA:
  We must give up the country to the barbarians!
  I wish to conquer Norway again!

COUNSELOR (*aside*):
  Bertha is mad! (*To* BERTHA:) Yes, your Majesty.

         (*Clarions are sounded.*)

Scene 9

A public place.

NORWEGIAN CITIZEN:
  They say Bertha will give us up to the barbarians!

SECOND NORWEGIAN CITIZEN:
  Impossible!

  (*The barbarian armies march in, with red and white
  banners.*)

BARBARIAN CHIEFTAIN: On to the Castle! Norway is
  Barbarian!

  (*Sounds of cannon.*)

Scene 10

The Throne Room.

MESSENGER:
  Bertha arrives, at the head of teeming troops!
  On her arrival from Scotland all Norway has rallied
    to her banner!
  Millions of Norwegians surround the castle shrieking,
    "Bertha, Queen of Norway!"

BARBARIAN CHIEFTAIN:
  Let us be gone! We cannot withstand such force.
  Quickly, to the tunnel!

  (*They disappear.*)

  (BERTHA *appears in regal splendor and walks to her
  throne, followed by applauding citizens. She ascends
  the throne.*)

BERTHA:
  Norway!

  (*She falls from the throne and lies dead in front of it.*)

NOBLE:
  Bertha is dead!

CITIZEN:

She was a great queen!

SECOND CITIZEN:

She conquered her own country many times!

THIRD CITIZEN:

Norway was happy under her rule!

(*Trumpets and sirens.*)

GEORGE WASHINGTON CROSSING THE DELAWARE

To Larry Rivers

Scene 1

Alpine, New Jersey.

GEORGE WASHINGTON:

> General Cornwallis, you cannot stay here in the trails of Alpine, New Jersey. The American army will drive you away, and away! Americans shall be masters of the American continent! Then, perhaps, of the world!

CORNWALLIS:

> What tomfoolery is that you speak, George Washington? You are a general, and generals are supposed to have a college education. No man with any sense would see a victory in this coniflct for any power but GREAT BRITAIN!

GEORGE WASHINGTON:

> General Cornwallis, I am a mild man, but you had

better not say that kind of thing to me. I tell you,
America shall win the Revolutionary War!

FIRST AIDE TO GEORGE WASHINGTON:
Our general speaks the truth, Englishman.

FIRST AIDE TO CORNWALLIS:
Do you dare to speak to General Cornwallis, im-
pudent Yankee?

FIRST AIDE TO GEORGE WASHINGTON:
Aye, I am an American, and I fear to speak to no man.

GEORGE WASHINGTON:
My aide is expressing the philosophy we all have.
It is bound to triumph over your own British authori-
tarian and colonial system. My men all see eye to eye
on this point.

CORNWALLIS:
I caution you, General Washington, that many of
them will never see eye to eye with anything again
if you persist in this useless, cruel, and wasteful battle.

GEORGE WASHINGTON:
Come, my loyal men. We waste our time in entreaty
with the English lord. He mocks us and all we believe.

FIRST AIDE TO GEORGE WASHINGTON:
Aye, General. I follow you.

OTHER AIDES: Aye, General, we come.

(*They leave.*)

CORNWALLIS:

There goes the greatest man who will ever live in America! If only he could come over to the English side, I could bring myself to give up my command to him. He is a perfect gentleman, excelling in manners as in speech. His dress is perfect, his buttoning neat, and his shoes of a high polish. He speaks frankly and freely, and will say straight out to his most bitter opponent that which is in his mind. There is nothing he could not accomplish, would he but set himself to it. What task, indeed, could ever challenge that general of the Revolutionary Army? He rides as he walks, with perfect grace; and when he reclines, one imagines one sees the stately bison taking its rest among the vast unexplored plains of this country, America, which now in foul and lawless revolt dares to lift its head against its English nurse and mother. What is more unnatural than that this man, Washington, who is one of God's gentlemen, should so defy the laws of right and wrong as to raise his hand against the breast that gave him suck, against the tender maternal care of England? O England, England! we who are your subjects are the most fortunate men on earth, and we shall struggle boldly to defend you, on land and at sea, no matter where we shall find ourselves, in whatever tempest or time of trouble that may come—we shall be, as we are, loyal to the end, and triumph we shall, for love makes our cause right. . . . But that man Washington!

(CORNWALLIS *leaves.*)

FIRST AIDE TO CORNWALLIS:

Our general is troubled.

SECOND AIDE TO CORNWALLIS:
   The sight of the Yankee general has quite o'erthrown
   him.

FIRST BRITISH SOLDIER (*cockney accent*):
   A did not think 'e was such a great man but I could
   'ave ho'ertopped 'im wi' my little musket 'ere. 'Tis
   bare gaddiness that our general be disturbed.

SECOND BRITISH SOLDIER (*cockney accent*):
   Aye, but disturbed 'e is.

THIRD BRITISH SOLDIER (*Irish brogue*):
   Come off, now. What is it turns your heads so low,
   and the sun beatin' back against them, and your steps
   draggin', and no light of day in your eyes, and here
   it bein' God's own glorious time, when His Majesty
   walked in the Garden of Eden, in the cool of the day,
   and the glorious messenger of Zeus almighty and the
   eye of friendly Apollo ashinin' and aglistenin' in
   yonder famous West, where so many of our victories
   has been? What is there to make a man sad in a time
   of day such as this is, when all is gold as far as the
   eye can listen, and where the buzzin' of a thrillion
   insects shines through the ear? If a man were not
   happy at such a moment, he were but half a man,
   and that half not much good neither, but only for
   changin' and blackin' the pots while old Mother helps
   herself to some kidneys. It is a glad song I would be
   singin' but for some that would have it that all men
   must be sad in the time of the American War. Saw
   you not General Washington?

FIRST BRITISH SOLDIER (*cockney accent*):
   Sawr 'im plain, I did, just as big as your 'ead there;

troubled a bit, our general is, 'aving seen 'im 'isself. Gaive a nice speech habout Hengland though.

SECOND BRITISH SOLDIER (*cockney accent*):
Aye, troubled 'e is, and deep, too. I see no good of this meetin'.

(*They all leave.*)

Scene 2

The American camp.

FIRST AMERICAN SOLDIER:
The General returns, and surely he will tell us much that he has seen.

SECOND AMERICAN SOLDIER:
When the General goes abroad, he never fails to tell each private soldier, though he be lowest in station in the entire Revolutionary Army, what he, the General, has seen, and what his thoughts have been upon the subjects of his contemplation.

THIRD AMERICAN SOLDIER:
Thus, each and every man in the Revolutionary Army shares in the secrets of the High Command, and every man knows exactly why he is fighting.

FOURTH AMERICAN SOLDIER:
This is democracy in action, actually being practiced in a military situation. The method of our struggle exemplifies its end—freedom for every man from the English.

FIFTH AMERICAN SOLDIER:
>   Here comes the General!

> (GEORGE WASHINGTON *enters and mounts a podium.*)

GEORGE WASHINGTON:
>   Friends, soldiers, and Americans, lend me your ears!
>   (*Laughter.*)
>   I have seen the British general, Cornwallis—
>   Brightly he shines in regal uniform,
>   And brightly shines his sword—but she will cut
>   No better, boys, than ours!
>   (*Draws his sword, amid the thunderous cheers of
>   the soldiers.*)
>   He said that we
>   Had not a chance at all to win the war. . . .
>   (*Laughter.*)
>   Let's show that Englishman how wrong he is
>   (*Growls.*)
>   And conquer them as quickly as we can! (*Cheers.*)

A RAGGED SOLDIER:
>   General Washington, how can we conquer the
>   Englishmen when we have no guns, no ammunition,
>   no clothing, and no food?

> (*Loud murmurs from the soldiers of* "Shhhhh shhh,"
> "Strike him," "Why does he want to spoil every-
> thing?" "Kill him," *etc.*)

GEORGE WASHINGTON (*unruffled*):
>   We must make raids—raids, raids,
>   Raids on the English supplies. We must make raids!
>   Raids for clothing and raids for food
>   To do the Revolutionary Army good;

Raids in the morning and raids at night,
Raids on our stomachs by candlelight,
Raids on the tea chest and raids on the mill,
Raids on the granary that stands by the hill;
Raids on the clothing tents, beautiful raids,
Raids on Cornwallis, and raids on his aides.
For stealing is licensed if for a good cause,
And in love and war, boys, you know there're no laws.
So pack up your shyness, your shame, and your fear,
And throw them away, and come meet me, all, here,
At twelve o'clock midnight, and off we shall go
To the camp of the English that lies down below!
And we shall return in their splendid attire,
And every man present shall have his desire.
So, come, get you ready—go blacken each face,
And meet me at midnight in this very place!

Scene 3

An English home.

ENGLISH GIRL:

You mustn't cry, Mummy. There's absolutely nothing
we can do. We are in England, and he is in America.
Your tears are going to waste. Has he written?

MOTHER:

The poor little fellow. I remember the first step he
ever took. His father, may his soul rest in peace, was
holding on to his tiny hands; and, when he began
to step forward, all by his little self, his daddy let
him go. And he took such a tumble! How I kissed
him then—oh!

ENGLISH GIRL:

I don't see why you keep having these morbid thoughts. Many soldiers return from wars unhurt, only to engage in some peaceful occupation in the pursuit of which they are killed by some unforeseeable accident.

MOTHER:

Oh!

ENGLISH GIRL:

Hugh is as safe in the army of General Cornwallis as he would be right back here at home. After all, General Washington's army is made up only of seedy criminals and starving bootblacks! They have neither food nor equipment, and everyone says it is not possible that they shall hold out for more than a few weeks against the skilled and well-equipped troops of our English army. In all probability the war has already ended in our favor, and but for the slow and sluggish meanders of the ships bringing the news, we should be cognizant of it this day, this very hour in which I must know the pain of seeing tears fall from your deeply beloved and old friendly eyes, Mother.

MOTHER:

Child, Artella, you are kind. But, dear, when a people fights for its freedom, even though its army be composed of little children bearing branches, that people will never stop until it has attained that freedom; so that it seems that, inevitably, that people will win, and Hugh, if he stay long enough, be, of necessity, wounded or killed, which is that at which I weep—

for nothing touches more nearly a mother's heart than the death of her only son.

ENGLISH GIRL:

But, Mother! the Americans cannot possibly win—they have no supplies!

Scene 4

The British camp at night. Complete darkness.

FIRST AMERICAN SOLDIER:

Jim?

SECOND AMERICAN SOLDIER:

Yes, Jack?

FIRST AMERICAN SOLDIER:

Jim, are you there, Jim?

SECOND AMERICAN SOLDIER:

Yes, Jack, I'm here, right here. What did you want, Jack?

FIRST AMERICAN SOLDIER:

Have you got some tobacco?

SECOND AMERICAN SOLDIER:

Yes. Here.

FIRST AMERICAN SOLDIER:

Thanks, buddy. It sure tastes good.

SECOND AMERICAN SOLDIER:
Isn't it delicious? I'm glad you like it.

FIRST AMERICAN SOLDIER:
It really is good.

SECOND AMERICAN SOLDIER:
I get a lot of satisfaction from hearing you say that.
Why don't you take a little more so you'll have some
for after the raid?

FIRST AMERICAN SOLDIER:
Aw, I don't want to—

SECOND AMERICAN SOLDIER:
No, go on, really, take it. I want you to have it.

FIRST AMERICAN SOLDIER:
Well, if you insist.

SECOND AMERICAN SOLDIER:
I do.

FIRST AMERICAN SOLDIER:
Thanks, Jim. You're . . .

SECOND AMERICAN SOLDIER:
Don't try to put it into words, Jack. Let's just forget it.

FIRST AMERICAN SOLDIER:
No—I . . .

SERGEANT (*cockney accent*):
Quiet up there! This is supposed to be a sneak raid.

GEORGE WASHINGTON:
What's the trouble here, Sergeant?

SERGEANT (*cockney accent*):
God save your Honor, hit's a couple of the men, Sir, 'as been talking more than what they ought to 'ave, and I was for putting them in line, Sir.

GEORGE WASHINGTON:
How long have you been in this country, Sergeant?

SERGEANT:
Two months, Sir. Not long. But I feel hit's as much my own country as if I'd been 'ere fifty years, your Lordship.

GEORGE WASHINGTON:
You wouldn't be a spy, by any chance, would you, trying to tip the enemy off by making noise?

SERGEANT:
Bless me, no, your Lordship, by all that's sacred and 'oly. I am but a poor soldier would do 'is best to make this a land for free men to live and trade in.

GEORGE WASHINGTON:
Very good. Continue with your work.

FIRST AIDE TO GEORGE WASHINGTON:
General Washington?

GEORGE WASHINGTON:
Is that you, Fitzdaniel? Haven't I told you not to use my name?

FIRST AIDE TO GEORGE WASHINGTON:

Begging your Worship's pardon, Sir, but I think we may have come on something, Sir. Here are many heads, arms, and legs, and if it is not the English camp, I know not what it might be.

GEORGE WASHINGTON:

Excellent. Every man on his stomach. Get away with everything you can. Food is most important. Next, ammunition and clothing. Whatever you do, make no noise. Kill no man unless absolutely necessary. Is that understood?

ALL (*whisper*):

Yes, General Washington.

(*Sounds of crawling about and scuffling.*)

CORNWALLIS (*in his sleep*):

What's that? Ho!

FIRST AIDE TO GEORGE WASHINGTON:

What was that noise?

SECOND AIDE TO GEORGE WASHINGTON:

The voice had a familiar ring.

FIRST AIDE TO GEORGE WASHINGTON:

Yes! it was Cornwallis.

SECOND AIDE TO GEORGE WASHINGTON:

Where does the English general lie?

FIRST AIDE TO GEORGE WASHINGTON:

Near us, most likely, since we heard him so clearly.

SECOND AIDE TO GEORGE WASHINGTON:
> Let's go into his tent. It is likely to be rich in booty!

THIRD BRITISH SOLDIER (*waking up; speaks with an Irish brogue*):
> Ooo-oooooooh me! (*Pause.*) Agh, it's little sleep I can be gettin', what with the cold wind blowin' against my head, and me all the time thinkin' of those that are near and those that are far away. And I did imagine as I lay thinkin' that I heard almost a rustlin', a kind of noise almost, as if the winds themselves had come to bring some news into our Irish camp. It's a little air I'll be needin', and out of my tent I'll be steppin' and lookin' at the fair face of the moon with all her tiny stars.

FIRST AMERICAN SOLDIER:
> What's this?

SECOND AMERICAN SOLDIER:
> It's a Limey, Jack.

FIRST AMERICAN SOLDIER:
> Shall we drop him?

SECOND AMERICAN SOLDIER:
> The General said no.

FIRST AMERICAN SOLDIER:
> Then what shall we do?

SECOND AMERICAN SOLDIER:
> Wait, and listen.

THIRD BRITISH SOLDIER:

Ah, 'tis a fair dark night, and such as it would be wrong to sleep through. There is beauty in the blackness of the sky, which bears not one tiny star. 'Twould be a fair night for a murder, and that's certain, for a man cannot see his hand before his face, even though he hold it up. A man could jump on another on a night such as this and sink a blade in his back without bein' noticed so much as a puff of smoke on a cloudy day. It's glad I am that the camp is guarded well by stalwart Irish soldiers and that we are safe from all harm.

SECOND AMERICAN SOLDIER:

Quick, into his tent!

FIRST AMERICAN SOLDIER:

Supposing he comes back?

SECOND AMERICAN SOLDIER:

Then we'll have to—

FIRST AMERICAN SOLDIER:

No!

SECOND AMERICAN SOLDIER:

Yes! But he may not come. Come on, Jack!

FIRST AMERICAN SOLDIER:

Lead the way!

GEORGE WASHINGTON:

Sergeant, tell the men that the object of the raid has been accomplished. We have more than enough supplies for the campaign. Have them reassemble here, and we will then depart for our own camp.

SERGEANT:

Yes, Sir. Yes, Sir. Oh, yes, Sir!

(*Much crawling and scuffling.*)

GEORGE WASHINGTON:

Men, the raid has succeeded. We return to the American camp tonight!

ALL:

Hurrah for General Washington!

Scene 5

The English camp, next day.

CORNWALLIS (*running out of his tent*):

Help! I've been robbed! My guns, my clothes, my food supplies—everything is gone!

FIRST AIDE TO CORNWALLIS:

And so have I! Everything is gone, everything!

SECOND AIDE TO CORNWALLIS:

And I.

THIRD BRITISH SOLDIER (*Irish brogue*):

And I.

COOK:

The kitchen tent is completely emptied of supplies!

QUARTERMASTER:
All our equipment and ammunition are gone!

ASSISTANT QUARTERMASTER:
And our clothing!

FIRST AIDE TO CORNWALLIS:
What shall we do?

SECOND AIDE TO CORNWALLIS:
Who has done this deed? It is impossible—

CORNWALLIS (*suddenly enlightened; is his calm self once more*):
Men, return to your quarters. Do not be alarmed. I shall issue instructions for your further conduct. Demoda and Bilgent, come with me.

(*All leave, save for* CORNWALLIS *and his two* AIDES.)

FIRST AIDE TO CORNWALLIS:
If it please your Grace, how—?

SECOND AIDE TO CORNWALLIS:
If your Lordship knows—

CORNWALLIS:
Precisely. It is very simple. The man Washington has duped us. In the dead of night, he and his soldiers must have crept into our camp and stripped us of supplies. It is the only possibility. The man is a genius! If only we could win him over to our side . . . I've got it! Bilgent, you were once on the stage. Go to my tent. There is one trunk there they did not

steal, because it was anchored to the ground. Take this key and open it. Inside you will find the uniform of an American officer. Put on this uniform and present yourself to General Washington, saying you have been sent to him by General Stevens, in Haskell. Then, when you have won his confidence, convince him of the justness of our cause. Washington is a righteous man, and if he is convinced we are right he will join us without hesitation. The future of England may depend on your mission! Take this key, and go!

(FIRST AIDE TO CORNWALLIS *leaves.*)

Now, Demoda, we must figure out a plan to obtain supplies. Our rear section is only three hours' march away, and we can easily reach them and resupply ourselves unless one thing happens—unless Washington is able to cut us off; and that he can do in one way only, by crossing a river—I forget its name. At any rate, there is little danger of his doing so, for he and his men are probably asleep after their strenuous night. Let's organize and march!

SECOND AIDE TO CORNWALLIS:
    Aye, aye, General.

Scene 6

The American camp. George Washington's tent.

GEORGE WASHINGTON (*sitting on his bed*):
    I am tired, and I need sleep. Good night, America.
    (*Lies down and sleeps.*)

(*A placard is now displayed, which reads THE
DREAM OF GEORGE WASHINGTON. Through-
out the dream,* GEORGE WASHINGTON *the man remains
sleeping on his bed, and the part of* GEORGE WASH-
INGTON *is played by a child actor.*)

GEORGE WASHINGTON:
   Where's Daddy, Mommy?

MOTHER:
   He'll be here in just a little while, dear. He's bringing you a present for your birthday.

GEORGE WASHINGTON:
   Oh, Mommy! A real present?

MOTHER:
   Yes, and you must thank him for it and be nice to
   your Daddy, as he loves you very much. Here he is
   now!

   (*Enter George Washington's* FATHER. *He is carrying
   a young cherry tree, which he gives to* GEORGE.)

FATHER:
   George, little George! Happy birthday to my little
   son!

   (GEORGE WASHINGTON *cries.*)

MOTHER:
   Why, baby, what's the matter?

GEORGE WASHINGTON:
   Oh, Mommy, you said it was so nice, but it's all dirty
   and covered with roots!

FATHER:

What's the matter with the little crybaby? Is he afraid of getting his hands dirty?

MOTHER:

Oh, Elbert, you promised! Be nice to the child. It is a little one yet.

FATHER:

Humph! He'll never amount to a hill of beans, I can guarantee you that. All right, Sister, give me back the cherry tree! I'll give it to some other kid in the neighborhood, one who's a real man!

GEORGE WASHINGTON:

Oh, Daddy, don't! Is it really a cherry tree?

FATHER:

Come on, let go of it!

MOTHER:

Let the child keep it, dear. He wants it. He was only frightened at first, because it was so dirty and covered with roots.

FATHER:

All right, all right, he can have it. But give it to me! You don't think it's going to grow in your hands, do you, you little squirt? These things have to be planted, you know.

MOTHER:

Elbert, don't be so sarcastic. George only wants to be sure that you will not give the tree to another child.

FATHER:

No, of course I won't! I got it to give to him, didn't I? I only said that about another boy because he acted like he didn't want it before, like it was something that was no good, something dirty.

MOTHER:

George, go with your Daddy and help him plant the tree.

GEORGE WASHINGTON:

Yes, Mommy.

(GEORGE WASHINGTON *and his* FATHER *plant the cherry tree, and both leave. Then* GEORGE WASHINGTON *comes back with a little axe and chops down the tree. The tree is carried off-stage, and once again all three members of the family appear.*)

MOTHER:

Oh, I'm so sorry to hear about that! I wonder who could have chopped it down?

GEORGE WASHINGTON:

I did, Mother. I cannot tell a lie.

MOTHER:

Oh, my darling! (*Hugs him.*)

FATHER:

What? You chopped down the tree I slaved for, you little brat? I'm going to give you the beating of your life!

MOTHER:

Elbert, please!

FATHER:

I'm going to give you a thrashing such as the world has never seen before!

GEORGE WASHINGTON:

I cannot tell a lie, but I can run! I can flee from injustice! The tree was mine, to chop down as I pleased!

FATHER:

I'll give you such a beating . . . !

(GEORGE WASHINGTON *runs off, his* FATHER *following him.* MOTHER *remains.* FATHER *returns.*)

FATHER:

He foxed me. He swam across the river. It was the only way he could have done it. The ONLY WAY!

(MOTHER *and* FATHER *vanish, as the "Dream" placard is removed.*)

GEORGE WASHINGTON (*waking up suddenly*):

Father! you help me now! Quickly, assemble the men! We march at once for the Delaware River!

Scene 7

A grayish-blue, flat area in front of the Delaware; the river cannot be seen. GEORGE WASHINGTON *enters at the head of his troops.*

FIRST AIDE TO GEORGE WASHINGTON:

We have marched quickly, and we have marched well. But what is the General's plan?

SECOND AIDE TO GEORGE WASHINGTON:

He has not confided it to me, but I have gathered from little things that he has said that it is to cross the Delaware and cut off Cornwallis' army in its search for supplies.

FIRST AIDE TO GEORGE WASHINGTON:

Washington is a genius! The army with supplies is the army that wins the war. Washington has planned everything just right. First our night raid, which took away all of their supplies; and now this forced march, to cut them off in their attempt to renew their supplies.

SECOND AIDE TO GEORGE WASHINGTON:

You speak well. Washington has planned our every step. See how nobly he marches at the head of our troops!

GEORGE WASHINGTON:

Halt! Here let us stop and dismount and prepare the boats.

(*Busy activity—dismounting, boat-building, etc. Enter* FIRST AIDE TO CORNWALLIS, *disguised as an American officer.*)

FIRST AIDE TO CORNWALLIS (*to* GEORGE WASHINGTON):

I come to you from General Haskell, Sir, who is hard-pressed at Stevens. I mean Stevens, Stevens, Sir, Stevens who is hard-hask at pretzelled, hart had at Prexelled, Sir, General Stevens, Sir, hart-passed at Haxel—

GEORGE WASHINGTON:

Tenwillet, remove this man at once to the medical

tent, and place him under armed guard. He seems dangerous.

SECOND AIDE TO GEORGE WASHINGTON:
Yes, your Worship.

FIRST AIDE TO CORNWALLIS (*being led away*):
The man is a genius! It is impossible to deceive him.

GEORGE WASHINGTON:
Fitzdaniel, what news is there of Cornwallis' army?

FIRST AIDE TO GEORGE WASHINGTON:
He advances quickly, Sir, but by crossing at once, Sir, we shall be ahead of him by half an hour.

GEORGE WASHINGTON:
Then let us go! For only if we go swiftly shall we have victory! And only victory is sweet! Come, men, battalions, uniforms, weapons, come, across the Delaware—we have nothing to fear but death, and we have America to win!

(*They go. Two* OLD MEN *enter. Both stare in the direction in which* GEORGE WASHINGTON *and his army have gone.*)

FIRST OLD MAN:
What do you see?

SECOND OLD MAN:
I am old, and I see nothing.

FIRST OLD MAN:
I hear something, as though the sound of splashing.

SECOND OLD MAN:

I hear nothing. My ears are dead things.

FIRST OLD MAN (*suddenly very excited*):

Why do I ask you what you hear and see, when now I hear and I see. Do you know what I hear and see?

SECOND OLD MAN:

No.

FIRST OLD MAN (*rapt*):

I see General George Washington crossing the Delaware, with all his troops and horsemen. I see him standing up in his boat, but I cannot make out the expression on his face. The men and horses on the other side of the river are shaking themselves free of water.

SECOND OLD MAN:

Go on! Do you see anything else?

FIRST OLD MAN:

No. Now everything is dark again.

SECOND OLD MAN:

What you saw was enough.

(*Cannons boom.*)

FIRST OLD MAN:

The American army has crossed the Delaware.

End

THE CONSTRUCTION OF BOSTON

This play was a collaboration with three artists: Niki de Saint-Phalle, Robert Rauschenberg, and Jean Tinguely. Once the construction of a city was decided on as a subject, Rauschenberg chose to bring people and weather to Boston; Tinguely, architecture; and Niki de Saint-Phalle, art. The people Rauschenberg brought to Boston were a young man and woman who set up housekeeping on the right side of the stage. For weather, Rauschenberg furnished a rain machine. Tinguely rented a ton of gray sandstone bricks for the play, and from the time of his first appearance he was occupied with the task of wheeling in bricks and building a wall with them across the proscenium. By the end of the play the wall was seven feet high and completely hid the stage from the audience. Niki de Saint-Phalle brought art to Boston as follows: she entered, with three soldiers, from the audience, and once on stage shot a rifle at a white plaster copy of the Venus de Milo which caused it to bleed paint of different colors. A cannon was also fired but did not go off. Niki de Saint-Phalle and Tinguely had doubles who spoke or sang their lines; Rauschenberg's lines were not spoken at all but were projected, at the appropriate times, on a screen.

NOTE: *After the opening dialogue,* SAM *and* HENRY *become the* CHORUS *and as such speak for a number of different personae. In the Maidman Playhouse production the two speakers alternated frequently—at the beginning of speeches, when there was a break in the course of a long speech, and usually at the beginning and end of quoted passages inside speeches—such as, for example, the statement by Beacon Hill in the first* CHORUS *speech.*

The scene is modern Boston. Backdrop of Boston buildings.

HENRY:
> Hello Sam.

SAM:
> Hello Henry.
> See where Boston stands so fair
> And cruel. Have you ever thought
> Once there was nothing there?

HENRY:
> I never thought of that!
> You mean there was mere space?
> No Milk Street, S.S. Pierce, and no South End?
> No place where the postman walks, no bend
> To turn toward Needham, waiting for one's date
> Or for one's fate, no building to sit in?

SAM:
> Well—even more—before the first man came to pass
> This site and called it "Boston," there was nothing—
> Merely grass and sea: three high hills called Tri-
> mountain:
> Beacon, Pemberton, Vernon,
> And the Salt sea—wallahhah!
> And the Cove.

HENRY:

And were there nymphs
Inhabiting this grove?
And demigods, and other treasure-trove
Of Ancient days?

SAM:

There were. They built this city.
Not ancient Botticelli
Nor sky-inspired Bellini
Ever trembled to
A sight more beautiful
Than Boston in her Ancient days
And during her creation!
They say men came then who were more than men,
Who from one market reared a whole town up,
Made urban weather to give urban dreams
Built high brick walls where once there flowed fresh
    streams.

HENRY:
Ah, fair to tell!

SAM:

Yet none were satisfied
Until one greater Spirit came, who changed
What they had done and made it beautiful.

HENRY:
What kind of Spirit?

SAM:
A woman—

HENRY:
Beautiful?

SAM:

Incredibly so—But

HENRY:

What is happening?

SAM:

—But now I feel faint

HENRY:

Everything is growing dark

A VOICE:

You speak of one men are not fit to know;
Such knowledge is not fit for mortal tongue.
Therefore this darkness. All must come again
As it has come before. You have undone
Three hundred years of building by your chatter
Of sacred things. This darkness signifies
Your crime; and your purgation shall be this:
You must see Boston built again
Just as it was before—perhaps, though, faster.
Oh tremble, mortals! Now, let there be nothing
But grass, Trimountain, and the answering sea!

(*Total darkness.*)

(*Lights go on. Boston has vanished.*)

CHORUS:

How strange! What freshness steals across my brow!
Delightful breezes, song of twittering birds,
And the faint smell of grass mixed with the spray.
See where the hawthorn blossoms, and the rose!
Ah in this wilderness let me remain

Forever! Here man's heart and brain find peace!
The year is 1630, peaceful year!
How lovely it is here!
And even nature seems to sing in joy!
Huge Beacon Hill cries out in gusty tones,
"How happy I am now, fat as a cow
And higher than a treetop's loftiest bough—
I'm made of mud and gravel
And squirrels up and down me travel
Which gladly I allow."
The light blue summer day
Reflected in Back Bay   (*Enter* RAUSCHENBERG.)
Shines like an eye—but stop—who comes here now?
Who is he? oh, what kind of man is he?

This seems to me no man, but more than man!
Hail, Populator. . . .
What shall you to this barren coastland do?

RAUSCHENBERG:
    Bring people!
    And manufacture weather for the people.

CHORUS:
    He hopes to have a city here—
    At least a little town—that's clear—
    Or else why bring the people down?

RAUSCHENBERG:
    That's clear. Here!

                    (RAUSCHENBERG *brings people*.)

CHORUS:
    He's bringing people.

RAUSCHENBERG:

 And weather too.

CHORUS:

 There is already weather.

RAUSCHENBERG:

  I'm bringing more. Cities need different weather than
   the country.
  Otherwise why would people go to the country? I'm
   bringing city weather here. I need it for the city.

CHORUS:

  Dark afternoons in autumn he
  Brings to Boston peerlessly
  And in winter with the hush
  Of evening, miles of snow and slush!
  Springtime warmth, exploding late,
  Daisies 'mid the fish and freight;
  Sultry summer afternoons
  To make the Boston citizens
  Dressed in high style, dressed to the tens,
  Uncomfortable as baboons—
  Oh where has our lovely climate gone?
  Ah Rauschenberg, have mercy!
  Yet it's lovely,
  And seems just right for Boston, I'll admit.
  I'd almost swear that I can hear
  The weather speaking as he brings it here
  To be a part of Boston—
  There is a deep gruff voice: "I am the storm!
  I have a lovely loud mellifluous form
  When I'm alone. Ah, but in the city
  Bumped against the fire escape,

Mailbox and wall, I lose my shape,
And lightning rods poke into me—
Oh let me be a storm at sea!"
"No, no," says Rauschenberg.
And now we hear the summer noon
Whose voice is rather like a croon:
"Ah in the country let me be!
Tall buildings are the death of me!
They block my light and make me black
And humid: sweat runs down my back!"
But Rauschenberg says, "Noon, march on."
And we hear the summer dawn
Complaining now to Rauschenberg:
"Bob, this transfer is absurd!
In the country redbirds sing
When they see me: everything
Cries aloud for joy! But here amid
The stench of fish and people
Black roadway and black steeple
What function can I serve? I like to please."

RAUSCHENBERG:

You shall, my tease,
My love, my delectation!
When you come
The city's heart shall, like a muffled drum,
Begin to beat, and as you go you'll see
Proffered to you constantly
Every single business day
A great urban-souled bouquet
Of people and their actions!

CHORUS:

That sounds fine! And now he brings divine

And holy moonlight, which says, "I
Am interrupted here," but Rauschenberg replies:
"So by your interruption shall you shine
More brilliantly and wake a million dreams
Instead of one: besides which, we need moonlight in
    the city."

RAUSCHENBERG:
    And now I have to stock
    The city up with people!

PEOPLE (*spoken by* CHORUS):
    We are Irish, we're Italian,
    We are British, why has he
    Brought us here to stock this city
    As if it were an aquarium,
    As if we were human fish?

CHORUS:
    Every city needs some people,
    And a racial mixture functions
    Very nicely in America.
    You should be glad to be together—
    Very exciting things will happen!
    Ah I can hardly restrain myself
    From singing praise to Rauschenberg
    When I see this racial mixture!
    How enthralling! How exciting!
    And, in the harbor, fish are biting!

RAUSCHENBERG:
    Now I think I've done—

CHORUS:
    All hail, great Rauschenberg!

RAUSCHENBERG:

And yet there's only one

CHORUS:

All hail to you!

RAUSCHENBERG:

Thing wrong. We have the weather and the people,
But they, the people, have no way to get
Out of the weather or back into it.
We need some BUILDINGS!

CHORUS:

Tinguely, spirit of the air,
Now descend, and kill despair!
Aid us with your mighty hands
Molding earth to your commands!
O spirit, come!

(TINGUELY *appears.*)

TINGUELY:

I am
Arrivèd!
Ah! what a lovely layout you have here!
What varied weather and what varied people!
What lovely mountains and what snappy sea!
I'll do it, Rauschenberg, for it inspires me!
Oh it sends great create-
Ive tremors all through me!

CHORUS:

All hail to Tinguely! We need houses to live in.

TINGUELY:

Peace, citizens—that's where I'll begin,
Quite naturally.

CHORUS:

Tinguely, we need public buildings.

TINGUELY:

Certainly! And ones with gildings—
That's my next endeavor!

CHORUS:

I have never
Seen such immense intense inflamed construction!
Oh like the beaver speeded at his work
Is Tinguely the great architectural Turk!
See how he functions! ah! ah!

TINGUELY:

But now we need more space!
How shall I solve this problem, tell,
For now we need more space!
Ha! Ha! I've got it! Now!

CHORUS:

Help, help!
My God, Tinguely, what are you doing? What are
you trying to do? What are you going to do?

TINGUELY:

The city needs more land area. Thus I am going to
fill the Mill Pond with the top of Beacon Hill. Two,
I am going to fill the Back Bay with sand, from
Needham, Mass. Thirdly, I am going to extend Boston
out into the harbor by means of docks.

CHORUS:

O brave ambition!
And see how he proceeds,
Ah mighty Tinguely!
Yet hear that cry
From Beacon Hill, which rends the sky,
"Oh do not dig me, Tinguely!
Oh Tinguely, leave me be!"
But he remorselessly
Goes digging on; and now he fills the Pond,
Which merely gasps, and now he smiles
To see poor Beacon Hill reduced by miles,
And now he turns another way
And contemplates the old Back Bay
And starts to fill it too.
At which the old Bay cries as to the skies:

"Boston, all that I can say
Is, it's grand to be a bay!
First you're full and then you're empty,
Then your friends go to the country—
They come back and fill you in:
All shall be as it has been.
Fill me up with sand and gravel,
No more boats across me travel—
And my chest where children play
Is black by night and brown by day.
Now I feel the sidewalks, clunk!
Slapping down on me, kerplunk!
And I feel the buildings rising
Filled with chairs and advertising
Where was once a boat capsizing,
Splashes, and a frightened brow—
There is nothing like that now!

Oh the buildings are so heavy—
How they weigh me down!"

Now you're the *town,*
Back Bay—you mustn't complain!
It's wonderful to be a part
Of an existent urban heart
Where on hot summer days
The heat sings its own praise
By sheer cement!

"I know that's true—
And I knew what you meant
Before you said it; still, my dear, do you
Know what it's like to feel upon your body
A seven-story home where there was only foam
Before? What used to be my shore
Ça ne l'est plus encore!"

TINGUELY:

Back Bay, you're lucky. You and Mill Pond are.
I am going to put
Sumptuous buildings on you that
Will make you lovely as a star.

CHORUS:

What? More?
What? More?

TINGUELY:

Come buildings, ah my airy darlings, come!

CHORUS:

They say he is a man, and yet he looks
Much like a woman to me. Yet he builds

Extremely like a man! They say his beard
Betrays his male identity, and yet—
And yet his skirt suggests he is a woman!
Perhaps this is an artist who combines
The sensitivity and strength of both
And is a whole man, such as Hesiod sung!
Oh man or woman, he can surely put
The buildings up! that noise of bumping fills
The atmosphere! and feel that weight upon us!

TINGUELY:

Now! now! I've done it! they are part of it!
Now to the seaside to fill in the sea!

CHORUS:

Fairest Tinguely, we the wharfs,
Splintery helpless wooden dwarfs,
Make appeal to you:
We love the water.
And if you'd be our friend, great building man,
O build us into her, thus let our natures
Sink down in her, oh let us fill the harbor
Till Boston's two times Boston's present size.

TINGUELY:

Sweet wharfs, I'm glad to see you are in love;
Your plan is just what I was thinking of.
Yes it's exactly what I thought about—
O bump bump bump throughout
The cove and harbor spread you out
Until we have a coastline that's in fact
A kind of wood and water pact,
A marriage of the forest to the sea!

CHORUS (*as water*):

What do I feel sink into me?

CHORUS (*as wharfs*):
    It's only we, dear harbor—
    Oh sweetheart, sister, mother!

CHORUS (*as water*):
    O close-clutched ecstasy!

TINGUELY:
    Well, wharf and water seem well satisfied—
    I hope the city will be too. Now what have I to do
    But plant a few more buildings here
    And then rush back to Scollay Square
    And, after, glance about
    To see what things I have left out—
    Ah, Commonwealth Avenue!
    I must make you, and then I've finished!

CHORUS:
    See how the smiling city takes its shape:
    Fair Scollay shining like a stem of grape;
    And Beacon Hill, though cut into,
    Still like an orange to the view
    Of one who sees it from Longfellow Bridge!
    O Tinguely, Rauschenberg, it's fine
    And yet I can't help feeling
    Something sublime is gone: pure nature; roses;
        sparrows singing; redbird; bluejay; twit-twit-
        twitter-twee!
    It seems such a short time ago we had that here!
    O tell me, how can we get back what's gone?
    I miss the fresh air and the lovely feeling!

RAUSCHENBERG:
    Don't you like cities? It's
    A fine time to ask me,

A fine time to bring *that* up!
Why Tinguely is already underground
                              (*thump thump*)
Building the subway, and you ask me how
To get back bubbling brooks?

CHORUS:

You don't know how?

                              (*Enter* NIKI.)

NIKI (*she sings*):

Well, I know how!
What this town needs is beauty, what Boston needs
     is art!
Let every heart rejoice,
Rejoice in every part
Of Boston!

                    (TINGUELY *emerges from the subway.*)

TINGUELY:

Wal, ze subway eez feeneesh.

NIKI:

But Boston is not quite.

CHORUS:

Men say she has a magic pistol
Which can turn plain glass to crystal
And can change an apple cart
To a splintery work of art!
Shooting at a person she
Makes him a celebrity!
Everything she does

Is not what it was—
Niki, bring us beauty's virtue!
Fire at that ancient statue—
Perhaps it has retained some value.

NIKI:

Here are streams—there are flowers
For the Public Garden's bowers! Let the flowers fall!

CHORUS:

O Niki de Saint-Phalle!
We knew that Boston could be beautiful,
But it was not until you came along.
Where were you, fairest of them all?

NIKI (*sings*):

Busy in Rome and Istanbul,
In Florence and in Paris;
Shooting landscapes in Shanghai
And portraits in Pekin;
Shooting rainbows in the sky,
Shooting the mosaics in
Saint Apollinaris.
I bring beauty and detail
By the shots which cannot fail
To delight the nation.
I make ugly statues fall,
And I give the palace wall
Lovely rustication.
I put features on the face
That is much too solemn;
I give a Corinthian grace
To the Doric column.
Why should I do anything
But be glad to make you sing

Praises to my shooting?
In my hand I have a gun,
And it is the only one
That gives columns fluting!
It's the only pistol which
Makes an empty canvas twitch
And become a painting!
It's the only gun that fires
Answers to the soul's desires—

CHORUS (*sings*):
Ah you are so pretty!

NIKI (*sings*):
Therefore on this summer night,
Citizens, for your delight,
I'll shoot up your city!

CHORUS (*sings*):
She'll shoot up the city.
(*Speaks:*)
There she goes!
From the top of old Beacon to the muddy Back Bay
There's a mumble of pleasure on this sunny day
As the shooting is heard to resound boom boom—
As the shooting is heard, like the cry of a bird,
And it's covering old Boston Ground
With love and pleasure.
Well, has she finished?

NIKI:
Yes.
And now, at last, my time is past, I must be drifting
homeward—
I go to treat art's plastercast, both Parisward and
Romeward!

Farewell, delicious citizens brought here
By Rauschen—Rauschen—what's his name?
    And dear
Great heavy streets of Tinguely, oh farewell!

CHORUS:
Now she drifts out to sea like a great bell!
How grand she is and fair!
We who feel our new creation
Run through us like syncopation
In the arms and tail
Praise her without fail!
Oh love which makes us new—
Newer than Rauschen—what's his name?—
Oh Niki, love for you,
It is which makes us new!
And like a nightmare which does not come true
This Boston now, which seems so old, is new
As if we saw the place for the first time
From the sublimest view-
Point: Mystic River Bridge—
And here is what we see, and it is beautiful,
Niki de Saint-Phalle, all because of you:
You have shot Boston full of love for you!
Ah, see how fair—
The outsize obelisk of Bunker Hill!

All hail to Tinguely for this masterpiece!
Below, on the left, the Boston Naval Shipyard,
Where Rauschenberg's creations slip
Beneath hot summer days he's given them
Up and down riggings of a full-rigged ship!
What sight so fair
As in this air

A seacoast made of ships!
To Rauschenberg then praise!
And there North Station, Beacon Hill,
Public Garden, swan with bill,
Restaurants where eat their fill
Fishermen and salesmen!
Here is Boston Latin tall,
There majestic Fanueil Hall,
Here's the Charles, and there's the Mall
And the Charles River Basin!
Who can count its beauties wholly?
Let us summarize them solely
Lest our praise proceed too slowly,
Niki dear, to you!

(TINGUELY *and* RAUSCHENBERG *kneel to* NIKI.)

TINGUELY:

Niki, all this city's buildings
With their warm old-fashioned gildings
I dedicate to you.

RAUSCHENBERG:

Niki, all these sunlit people
Or in shadow of a steeple
I consign to you.

NIKI:

And yet without you two, what could I do?
We must have people and they have to live
Inside of something: therefore I shall praise
You equally, for fashioning this maze!
For I cannot exist without the rest
Of life, although I am perhaps what's best.

Now, citizens, sunset cover you
Oh fairest sunset cover you
Now fairest Boston mother you and cover you and
    smother you, fair Boston cover you,
(*Sings:*)
And until then, ADIEU!

End

SIX IMPROVISATIONAL PLAYS

THE ACADEMIC MURDERS
A Play of Detection, with Improvisations

Scene 1

The office of Department Chairman AUERHEIM, *a stout tweedy man in his late forties. His secretary,* MISS FUND, *sits typing in the office just outside. Enter a tall young man of about twenty-five; not seeing him at first,* MISS FUND *is a little startled.*

MISS FUND:
Ah—!?

FETHERING:
I'm George Fethering. I have an appointment to see Professor Auerheim.

MISS FUND:
Oh—yes—of course. Just a moment. (To AUERHEIM:)

Sir, there's a young man to see you—Mr. Fethering.

AUERHEIM:

Oh yes—uh—show him in.

MISS FUND:

You can go right in, Mr. uh—

FETHERING:

Fethering. Yes. Thank you.

AUERHEIM:

Well, Mr. Fethering, what can I do for you?

FETHERING:

I would like to apply for a job in your department, sir.

AUERHEIM:

Yes. I understand from your letter that you are quite
a Yeats scholar.

FETHERING:

That's right, sir. I don't want to boast, but I dare
say there's nothing about W. B. Yeats that I don't
know. Nothing except what may be contained in the
"secret letters," of course.

AUERHEIM:

The "secret letters" . . . ? Hmmm. I don't know anything about those. What are they?

FETHERING:

They are a group of letters kept in the possession of
the heirs of Lady Gregory, sir. Yeats' will contains a

stipulation that they are not to be opened for a thousand years.

AUERHEIM:

That seems rather a long time to keep something secret.

FETHERING:

Yes, sir. But apparently they contain information which Yeats thought might be harmful in our time. He believed that if the world was hardy enough to last for another thousand years probably nothing could harm it.

AUERHEIM:

It seems an ingenious idea . . . Well, let's get down to business. You have your degree, do you not?

FETHERING:

Yes, sir, a Ph.D. from the University of Minnesota. I worked there with Hocking T. Nott on my dissertation on A.E., George Russell.

AUERHEIM:

The letter from Nott praised you very highly indeed. I vaguely remember reading the abstract of your dissertation, but I don't remember too well what it was about. Could you refresh my memory?

FETHERING:

If you put your memory on the table, sir, I may be able to refresh it.

AUERHEIM:

Mr. Fethering! What on earth do you mean?

FETHERING:

I'm sorry, sir. I—I guess I'm just a little nervous. When I am, I often make clumsy remarks of that kind. I have been reading a lot about Zen Buddhism, sir, and that sort of remark just naturally comes to my mind when I am nervous.

AUERHEIM:

I see. I see. Do you know Jung's splendid introduction to Suzuki's *Introduction to Zen Buddhism?*

FETHERING:

Yes, sir. I think Jung rather misses the point, sir. He tends to make Zen awfully Jungian.

AUERHEIM:

Ummm. Yes. Perhaps. It may be that I simply prefer the thought of Jung to that of Suzuki and the Zen masters.

FETHERING:

Sir, you should never say a thing like that!

(AUERHEIM *dies.*)

(*Improvised speech by* FETHERING *on the danger of attacking Zen.*)

Scene 2

The same office, twenty minutes later. Enter Police Officer STRAITER *and his assistant, Patrolman* BUDGE.

STRAITER:

So this is the murderer!

FETHERING:

Sir, I didn't touch the victim. Miss Fund can testify to that.

MISS FUND:

I didn't see a thing. I was busy here in my office with my typewriter.

FETHERING:

Sir, if Miss Fund won't admit that she was spying on us, you are free to examine the body for finger-prints.

MISS FUND:

Oh! poor Professor Auerheim! What have you done to him, you horrible person?

STRAITER:

Young lady, don't become hysterical. If this man is the murderer, we shall certainly see that he gets what he deserves. As yet, however, we really have no evidence.—Very well, Budge, you stay here and see that no one disturbs the body. I am going to phone our scientific squad to get over here on the double and examine this body for fingerprints.

BUDGE:

Yes, sir.

Scene 3

A political hall.

STRAITER:

Since there is no evidence of the body having been touched, it looks as though you're free, Fethering. But don't leave the city. We shall be wanting to have you within reach at all times for questioning.

FETHERING:

Sir, is that legal?

STRAITER:

You're damn right it is, Fethering. If we wanted to, we could hold you as a material witness indefinitely. In fact, I have half a mind to clap you in jail right now for your improper question.

FETHERING:

Oh no, sir. Yes, sir. I understand. I was just asking. You see, I know nothing of the law.

STRAITER:

Very well, Fethering. You are dismissed.

Scene 4

Fethering's furnished room.

FETHERING:

It would have been foolish to tell the police officer what I think actually killed Auerheim. My own problems, meanwhile, are only redoubled by this whole affair.

(*Improvisation by* FETHERING *on the difficulties of his life, his unpleasant early childhood, his need for a job, etc., and his determination to go to Japan to try to get to the root of the mystery.*)

Scene 5

Japan.

Improvisation of a busy day of turmoil in the Tokyo streets.

At the end, enter FETHERING.

Scene 6

The prison room of a ship, sailing to the United States. FETHERING *behind bars.*

POLICE OFFICER:

We told you not to leave the city, Fethering.

FETHERING:

But, sir, I did it only to try to get to the heart of the mystery—

POLICE OFFICER:

> If you expect us to believe *that*, then you are a greater fool than we thought!

Scene 7

Above, in the ship's bar. POLICE OFFICER, *other policemen, and other passengers.*

Improvisation: Discussion of how great a fool FETHERING *is to expect them to believe such a story. At the end, enter* RADIO MAN.

RADIO MAN:

> Look! look! listen! There may be some truth in what the boy says after all! The University of Blenheim has just exploded!

POLICE OFFICER:

> Blenheim!? What in tarnation has Blenheim got to do with this case? Constantia University, where Professor Auerheim was murdered by this boy, is in New York.

RADIO MAN:

> But wait—wait—listen to this—Bleinheim, my dear police officer, is the city in which Dagobert von Auerheim was born!

SAILOR (*rushing up from below*):

> And listen to this! The ship has been disembowelled, and young Fethering has mysteriously escaped. He can't be found anywhere!

POLICE OFFICER:

But then we must be sinking!

ALL:

Help! ho! Man the lifeboats! Abandon ship! Ho!

Scene 8

A lovely dusky garden in Japan. FETHERING *and a beautiful young Japanese girl,* TACOCA.

FETHERING:

I hope you don't mind my telling you this tedious story?

TACOCA:

I don't find it tedious at all, my darling. I don't find anything that you say tedious.

FETHERING:

To think, that I once planned to be a teacher!

TACOCA:

Yes—and that now you know what your true destiny is—to be a MAN!

FETHERING:

Yes, but I would still like to know who killed Professor Auerheim.

TACOCA:

We can ask at the shrine after we have performed

our ablutions. But meanwhile, here comes my father, the famous Japanese business man.

(*Enter* TACOCACOM, *a huge burly man.*)

TACOCACOM:
Hello, son! Been hearing a lot about y—

(*He drops dead.*)

Curtain

(*Improvised* EPILOGUE *by Tacoca.*)

End

EASTER

Scene 1

A large lovely lawn filled with Easter eggs. Children roll-
ing the eggs, etc. Improvisation by children on why they
like Easter. The scene ends with a symphony orchestra
playing something well-known from *Parsifal*.

Scene 2

A cave in the mountains. At the mouth of the cave stand
a number of very large Easter Rabbits. Improvisation:
they discourse on the pleasures and burdens of Easter
from the rabbits' point of view. The scene ends with very
thunderous music, probably from Berlioz.

Scene 3

A church. A number of priests are gathered informally
about the altar and the lowered area in front of it. Improvisation: they discuss the meaning of Easter to church
and to churchman, their love of the ecstatic aspects of the

holiday, their eagerness in awaiting it, but also their displeasure at the pagan aspects of the popular Easter myth as well as at the general commercialization of the holiday by stores and popular media of communication. The scene ends with a number of grand opera bassos and baritones singing popular songs.

Scene 4

Empty stage. Improvisation: a murder is committed. The police arrest the criminal and electrocute him. The scene ends with low, solemn death-march music.

Scene 5

The resurrection. Entire improvisation. After the resurrection the stage fills up with the actors, who discuss the meaning of the play. Finally they are drowned out by extremely loud noises of coughing.

Curtain

MEXICO CITY

An elderly American homosexual tries to describe Mexico City to an illiterate and extremely ugly Finnish farm girl who has never been in any city whatsoever. He should try to be as complete in his description as possible, including such things as streetcars, buses, hotels, markets, and so on, as well as the life pattern of ordinary persons of the various social classes in the city. When he has finished (his description should take from fifteen to forty-five minutes), the farm girl should try to repeat everything he has said to her with as much exactitude as she can manage. When she has done so, the elderly man should tell her to what extent he feels she has truly captured the spirit and mood of the city.

THE LOST FEED

Seven actresses, impersonating hens and chickens, should, while retaining their human modesty and dignity, act out in as chicken-like a way as possible the drama of the lost feed. The feed for the day is missing. None of the hens or chickens present is responsible for the absence of the feed, but each one suspects that some one of the others on-stage may be the culprit. Whatever the hens and chickens do, they should make no strictly *personal* remarks when they accuse one another. Their accusations should be rather flat and rather general, accusations which could be leveled at anybody about just about anything. Chicken life is not thought to be very differentiated. After the chickens and hens have been arguing for a long time, the feed should be brought in and given to them.

THE GOLD STANDARD

A Mountain Shrine, in China. Two Monks enter, and try, without the slightest success, to explain the gold standard to each other, for four hours. There should be nothing comical whatsoever in anything they say. The drama should be allowed as a "field day" for the lighting technician, who should be allowed, and even encouraged, to make as many changes of lighting to show time of day, season, atmosphere, and mood as he deems fitting so as to make the play as beautiful and meaningful as it can possibly be. The play should end with a snowfall and with the exit of the Monks.

COIL SUPREME

Eight or ten actors come on stage, being anyone they want. They speak for thirty minutes. The only requirement is that every sentence they utter must contain the phrase "coil supreme." They may distort the language in any way they wish in order to do this. They should try to generate as much excitement as possible by what they say and do, and the play should end on a note of unbearable suspense.

THE RETURN OF YELLOWMAY

Enter YELLOWMAY.

YELLOWMAY:
　　Oh I have surfeited so many borders
　　Seeking for an equitable light!

CROWD:
　　Welcome back, Yellowmay!

　　　　　　　　(*A huge light bulb is brought in.*)

YELLOWMAY:
　　Here will I proclaim my new religion!
　　Guinevere shall be the Queen of April

　　　　　　　　　　(GUINEVERE *dances in.*)

And I myself shall be the God of May.

　　(*Thunder and explosions. The seashore.*)

　　(*Enter* KING LEAR.)

LEAR:

You see me here, you Gods, a poor old man
More sinned against than sinning.

CHORUS OF GODS:

Yes, we see you, Lear.

(*Enter* YELLOWMAY.)

And also we see Yellowmay!

(*A Dome is brought in.*)

YELLOWMAY:

I here declare my new politick power.
Here shall I stay to manage all the state!

(*Crowds cheer. The Ocean is revealed. With a* SEA-
BIRD.)

SEABIRD:

I am worried about Yellowmay. I am wondering
If he should not practice more modest ambitions.
He is likely to get in trouble with
The real gods and political powers, behaving
As he's been behaving these days.

(*The City of San Francisco.*)

(*Enter a* WALRUS, *with* YELLOWMAY.)

WALRUS:

San Francisco, welcome your new ruler,
And welcome to his queen of pretty May.

(GUINEVERE *is drawn in in a flowery cart.*)

YELLOWMAY:

I do believe she is my queen, my heart!

(*Honolulu.*)

RULER:

Here in this new state,
Yellowmay, may you and Guinevere
Be happy, wearing the traditional Hawaiian lei.

(*They put them on.*)

YELLOWMAY:

Thank you, sir. And might we now
Visit that famous leper colony?

RULER:

You shall.

(*They go off.*)

(*Leper Colony.*)

YELLOWMAY:

Lepers! I am Yellowmay!

LEPER WOMEN:

Kill him! kill him!

LEPER MEN:

No, preserve him, save him for our sanctuary!

RULER:

Be careful! What sanctuary do you lepers have, any-
way?

LEPERS:

Our leprosy sanctuary! Now clear out of the way!
We want him!

(*They capture* YELLOWMAY *and lead him away.*
RULER *rages, and* GUINEVERE *weeps.*)

(*Absolute darkness. Four years later.*)

ELEPHANT:

Rescue by the animals

GIRAFFE:

Is hard but not hopeless—

KANGAROO:

We will rescue Yellowmay

HIPPOPOTAMUS:

If Guinevere permits us.

(*Enter* GUINEVERE, *wearing a dress and a crown of
green flowers.*)

GUINEVERE:

No, animals, do not rescue Yellowmay
You only would yourselves be put in prison.
And something there is happening of great
      importance.
Some day he'll be free.

(*Her flowers fade. It is autumn.*)

(YELLOWMAY, *crowned King of the Lepers, in a
purple crown and on a yellow throne.*)

YELLOWMAY:

King of the Lepers, I—
Who once wanted to be king of the world.
And yet I feel this kingdom is the essential one, I feel

(LEPERS *come in and do a ceremonial dance. They present* YELLOWMAY *with a young girl and he kills her. The* LEPERS *quietly carry her off.*)

That this is the essential kingdom of our time.

(*The Jungle floats away, revealing* YELLOWMAY *lying asleep on the beach.* GUINEVERE, *wearing the head of a Seabird, leans over him.*)

GUINEVERE:

Darling, wake up.
Bad dreams of leprosy oppress the night—
Wake up.

YELLOWMAY (*still lying down*):

Nothing that happens
Affects the human heart
But sadness.

GUINEVERE:

Now the curtain rolls away!

(*It does—revealing the city of Paris and crowds.*)

CROWD:

We declare Yellowmay King of the World!

(YELLOWMAY *stands up. The* LEPERS *come in and he goes off with them.*)

(*Silence, music, end.*)

THE REVOLT
OF THE GIANT ANIMALS

KANGAROO:
Here shall we,

GIRAFFE:
Revolting animals,

HIPPOPOTAMUS:
Gather our forces by the sea

ELEPHANT:
To war on Master Yellowmay.

(*Enter* YELLOWMAY *and* GUINEVERE, *in a Royal Cart.*)

YELLOWMAY:
To thee I do bequeath these kingdoms, sweetest—
May they lie upon your heart
Gently as a peanut.

GUINEVERE:
Yellowmay, look! turn around!

YELLOWMAY:

It's the giant animals, in revolt!

End

THE BUILDING OF FLORENCE

Florence.

GIRAFFE:
　　Come, lolly counselors, here are your plans.

ELEPHANT:
　　They say the competition for the Dome is fierce.

KANGAROO:
　　Tell me what competition is this.

HIPPOPOTAMUS:
　　It is a competition for the Dome of Florence,
　　Celebrated Duomo,
　　Which we are now building.

GIRAFFE:
　　Who's favored to win the prize?

ELEPHANT:
　　Michelangelo, of the brilliant blue eyes?

HIPPOPOTAMUS:
   No, he's only a baby as yet.

GIRAFFE:
   Though he'll design the Laurentian Library of great
      fame, you can bet!

KANGAROO:
   And other masterpieces of enormous size.

HIPPOPOTAMUS:
   I have been reading the Autobiography
   Of Benvenuto Cellini . . .

GIRAFFE:
   That's a good book—

ELEPHANT:
   Here is Florence in its period of formation.

GIRAFFE:
   And yet we live after Dante does.

HIPPOPOTAMUS:
   Not if our creator wished to transform us
   And transfer us to another period . . .

GIRAFFE:
   Do you think he would do that?

ELEPHANT:
   We're speaking of holiei
   Things perhaps than men should speak of—

HIPPOPOTAMUS:

Be quiet! I hear a cry!

(*It becomes darker. Enter the* ARNO RIVER—*it may be* YELLOWMAY *in disguise.*)

ARNO:

I am the famous Arno River
Which water to wonderful Florence supplies—
But have you thought of me at night, in dark,
How lonely and how odd I am . . . ?

GIRAFFE:

Good Lord! I hear a bird!
And you are the river of time as well!

(*Rush!! everything is blown off-stage, or gotten off somehow. Bright sunlight. The year 1266.*)

MAN:

They say a new baby's been born in our town—

SECOND MAN:

Yes, Dante Alighieri of famous renown.

MAN:

But who are these figures who walk toward us now

SECOND MAN:

Who seem of another age, bent the Lord knows how!

GIRAFFE, HIPPO, ELEPHANT, KANGAROO:

Oh alas alas!
We are that famous Arno, that flows unrecognized
In its true nature, and we

Are principally what isn't known about time,
And it's also true that death we are . . .

ELEPHANT:

Do you want information from the future? I have it
now!

LORENZO DE MEDICI:

There's no time for that now! Here is Dante!

(*Baby Dante is brought out on a silken cushion. Behind him, painted on a flat, is a Florentine crowd,
principally ladies resembling those in the Dante and
Beatrice "recognition scene."*)

GIRAFFE:

Gosh, Elephant, it's Dante!

RULER:

Think of all this baby has to do!

(*Enter, unobserved,* YELLOWMAY, *who shoots Baby
Dante.*)

YELLOWMAY:

Nothing that the future
Holds in store can be—

(YELLOWMAY *is shot by Florentines. The Animals go
to pick him up and take him off. They discover his
River costume.*)

ELEPHANT:
Why—it's the Arno!

KANGAROO:

From this day forth it will never be the same—

GIRAFFE:

On some future day

HIPPOPOTAMUS:

It will run dry.

(*Procession off-stage.*)

End

Scenes from
ANGELICA

*The main characters in the opera are three Spirits, who
cause much of what happens in France in the nineteenth
century: Angelica, the Spirit of Beauty; Edouard, the Spirit
of Change and Civic Progress; and Jean, the Spirit of Art.
At the beginning of the century (also the beginning of
the libretto) Angelica loves Edouard, but in the succeed-
ing years Jean wins her love through the creations of Romantic art and poetry. Desperate to regain her affections,
Edouard searches for a man who can redesign Paris in
such a way as to make it irresistible to her. He finally finds
Haussmann, who, as Prefect of the Seine under Napoleon
III, was the creator of modern Paris. The scenes included
here show Haussmann's successful reconstruction of the
city. The scenes are Scene 6 of Act I and Scenes 3, 4, and
8 of Act II. In the last act (which follows the triumph of
Haussmann), Angelica finds the choice between the creations of the two Spirits impossible to make—for by the
end of the 1890's Jean has brought about Impressionist
painting and the poetry of Rimbaud and Mallarmé, and
Edouard has changed life on earth by bringing into exist-
ence electric power and new means of transportation such*

as the automobile. Unable to give her love exclusively
either to Jean or to Edouard, despite a prophecy that the
world may be destroyed if she fails to choose one of
them, Angelica determines to leave the earth and go to
the Kingdoms of the Air, where she will remain until she
can make a decision. The opera ends with her departure
and with the beginning of the twentieth century.

The Courtyard of the Sorbonne. EDOUARD *observing the*
students who pass by.

EDOUARD:
    Oh I must find a man to build up Paris—now, help
        me, great Sorbonne!
    That from your many classes I find one
    Who has the strength of will to do
    What I have got to do:
    Change Paris to a star,
    And so win back Angelica to me!
    And yet I need a special kind of man—
    One not too up to date! . . .
    Oh always in the past
    Art has all been for the state—
    Like the lovely Parthenon
    Those great statues walk upon—
    The Aeneid: a state purchase;
    The frescoes in a million churches—
    Titians brighter than the dawn
    In city halls—Need I go on?
    But today some strange new consternation
    Has brought about a different situation:
    Artistic separation!
    Poets looking at religion
    Where it's fallen like a pigeon,
    Recommend instead creation,

Freedom, gloomy bouts with hell,
And a woman's human smell
Mixed with musk and ambergris!
What are such as they to me!
Bards without one moral tenet—
Who could read them to the senate?
Painters wild as waterfalls—
Picture them on courthouse walls!
And all inspired by this proud new spirit
Who took Angelica
And calls himself "Romantic"—I can't endure it!
Oh I still have the power of the grand,
The huge, enormous, simple, overwhelming,
Tremendous, great, self-evident, controlling
Sweet, clean, and pure objective mighty city,
State, and empire, the tremendous beauty
Of the external truth set up by man—
Oh let him walk with Beauty if he can!
Oh let him walk with Beauty for a while—
I'll change the streets in which they pause and smile!
I'll change the buildings that they walk into
And when they exit I'll have changed the view!
I'll tear down places that they love the best
As part of a great stylish movement West—
No more dark streets about the Place Maubert:
I'm going to fill this city with fresh air!
Fresh air and movement, fountains, air and light—
Then Beauty never can escape my sight!
Nor will she wish to—What is greater than
Free space and light? But I must find a MAN!

(*Enter* HAUSSMANN.)

HAUSSMANN:
Farewell, students, friends, farewell!

STUDENTS:
>Farewell, Georges Eugène Haussmann!

EDOUARD:
>It is he!
>The very man I need—ah, Haussmann! Haussmann!
>Haussmann, genius, take from me
>Such immortal energy
>That this Paris which appears
>So unchanging where it stands
>You'll rebuild in nineteen years
>With your mighty prefect's hands!
>Take from me the strength, the joy,
>To construct and to destroy!

HAUSSMANN (*pausing as he walks*):
>Ah, into my brain come flooding
>Visions, mighty change foreboding,
>Things I shall accomplish when
>I am Prefect of the Seine.
>Prefect of the Seine—oh, no!
>Never so high can Haussmann go!
>What a strange exotic dream
>And yet it seemed to me it had a true prophetic
>   gleam!

(HAUSSMANN *starts to walk on, then stops again.*)

>Yes, I could have sworn that I
>Saw against the pink-blue sky
>Of a Paris afternoon
>An opera house like a balloon,
>And in front, until the quai,
>Buildings shoved out of the way
>Making for the happy few

An impressive Avenue!
And I heard the pleasant roll
Of the word "Sebastopol,"
As if a boulevard could go
In the rain and in the snow
From the Seine into the wilderness—
Nor did I hear "Boulevard St.-Michel" less!
I heard them all and burn to do
What a man has got to do,
Make his city fresh and new,
Though half torn down and tunneled through,
Each thing he touches beautiful and new!

(HAUSSMANN *leaves.*)

EDOUARD:

And now to get an autocratic government
So Haussmann can perform his task unbothered—
Away to England! Louis Napoleon's there—we'll see
what things shall be!

(*He leaves.*)

❃ ❃ ❃ ❃ ❃

Vieux Quartier, Street and Place. Old Building with Gargoyles.

EDOUARD:

Oh see where Haussmann comes, see where he comes
To put these projects into execution!
See how he moves as to the sound of drums,
Intent on architectural revolution!
His light militia carry pick and hammer
To rob the city of its old, and give it a new glamor!

See where he comes, see where the Baron comes!
Oh he shall win Angelica back
For if she isn't blind
She'll like the breezy Paris he creates!
See where he comes with compass, cranes, and
    weights!

(*Enter* HAUSSMANN, *with Workmen of the Second
Empire.* EDOUARD *leaves. Workmen work.* HAUSSMANN
gives orders.)

HAUSSMANN:

Here, put that building back, it's sticking out
A good three inches farther than the rest!
What do I care if it's the Hotel Vair?
Chop off the front so that it evens up!

GARGOYLES:

Oh, do not chop us off! we ancient statues
Are beautiful and fine and full of meaning!

HAUSSMANN:

What? do these houses sing? Chop off the front!

GARGOYLES:

Oh, do not chop us off! we ancient statues
Are beautiful and firm and full of love!

(*Two lovers appear on a balcony.*)

GIRL:

I love you, darling! Oh! look what they're doing
To the façade of lovely Hotel Vair!
There is no faith nor truth, not anywhere!

MAN:

Except in these my arms!

GIRL:

But oh look there!

MAN:

Do not look, dear. There is a constancy
Undreamed of by this dull, proud Huguenot!

(*They retire from the balcony.*)

HAUSSMANN:

I heard you, lovers. Oh, my heart is sick
Sometimes, and I am full of indecisions!
These gargoyles, I suppose, are beautiful,
Although they surely don't appeal to me!
But when I think of Rome and when my nose
Is filled at intersections by fresh air,
At intersections by fresh air,
Oh, then I know what Paris ought to be!

(*Enter* ANGELICA, *who watches.*)

Paris should be like a star,
Shining near and not afar,
Paris should be like a star!

Every avenue a beam
From the center of a dream—
Every avenue a beam—

Paris should be filled with air,
Interstellar spaces where
Everything is clear as air!   (*Enter* JEAN.)
Paris!

CROWD OF WORKMEN:

Hurrah! for the new Paris!

HAUSSMANN:

But now beneath the street I hear
A sweet music gently clear—
As I walk, my soul's seduction—
The gay sound of sewer construction!
Imperial workmen, to your labor!
I shall join you somewhat later.
Here is an entrance—here!

(*He descends.*)

CROWD:

Hurrah!

JEAN:

See how affairs come to a head!
Haussmann wins the crowd's approval—
We must work for his removal!
He is making Paris
Hideous to see!
Ignoring all the talent of my artists,
What does he use for artists?
Academic Bonapartists!
Wrecking in a single day
Our great Ile de la Cité,
Tearing down its ancient alleys
Narrow and marine as galleys
With their beautiful buildings, which
Like great sailboats turn and pitch.
Oh, repellent day!

ANGELICA:

    Oh, and yet there is
    Excitement in this plan of his
    To make all Paris like a star—
    To shuffle little streets like cards
    And deal them out as boulevards,
    Avenues shining straight and wide
    With a park on every side,
    Brilliant streets which radiate
    At a white and lovely rate
    To Denfert or Passy slim as a bar!
    Woods at Boulogne and Vincennes
    And at Buttes-Chaumont for workingmen,
    And underground fresh running streams
    To bring sweet odors to sweet dreams—
    Oh tell me if there are
    More lovely plans than these to change a city?

JEAN:

    Well, you only see one side of it—
    Let's go!

                      (*They leave.*)

Sewer with Sewer Boat, HAUSSMANN *being rowed along by* OARSMAN.

OARSMAN:

    Dee dee dum, dee dee dum, etc.

HAUSSMANN:

    Oh as we go sailing down the sewer

Everything seems beautiful and pure,
For this sewer is not used as yet
And in its pleasant oval we forget
As we watch the oarsman's steady arm
Everything but its esthetic charm!

Where else on the planet can be found
Miles of walled-in river underground?
Where can one sail in a boat this way
And never see the light of night or day,
But only feel them, as one feels a love
For things beyond, most certain, pure, above?

Oh may all Paris soon be served by these
New sewers, and may the sweet Paris breeze
Be sweeter for their taking all away
Underground, forever, night and day!
Oh may our sewage problem soon be gone!
May Paris be a star! Oarsman, row on!

❋   ❋   ❋   ❋   ❋

Rive Droite: wide Avenue, with Place.

ANGELICA:

Oh Edouard, it *is* beautiful!
Bois de Boulogne, Champs Elysées . . .

EDOUARD:

Yes, I knew what you would say—
For, my love, without your aid
All this could not have been made!
Though you had rejected me
Souls do more than men can see,

And, although you'd left me, dear,
I would feel your presence here—
So that what you see, you are,
Drenched in brightness like a star.

ANGELICA:

I was here with you?

EDOUARD:

You were.
See those markets that we built
And that dome, all iron and gilt,
Modern art to banish gloom
From the library reading room—
Here, the opera; there, you see
The long rue de Rivoli;
There, the Annex to the Louvre
Round which the *calèches* move . . .

ANGELICA:

I don't like that addition much.

EDOUARD:

Well, I did not feel your touch,
To tell the truth, when we did that.
Which makes me remember that
Haussmann, to whom we owe so much,
Is not with us at this hour!

ANGELICA:

I heard that he had been dismissed
From power—

(*Enter* HAUSSMANN.)

HAUSSMANN:

> Alack! thrown down!
> Paris should be like a flower,
> And each petaled avenue—
> Ah, sweet Prefect, can you sing
> When you are losing everything?
> When Napoleon, compromising
> (Which is not at all surprising)
> In order to preserve his crown,
> Has agreed to cast you down?
> Paris, Paris, was it fated
> I'd not be appreciated?
> Ah, sweet Prefect, can you sing
> When you are losing everything?

EDOUARD:

> Haussmann, sing! be glad! rejoice
> With a more than human voice!
> Haussmann, genius, take from me
> Such immortal energy
> That even in your darkest hour
> You feel the beauty and the power
> Of all that you have done. And know
> Capitals round the earth shall grow
> Upon this model Paris you have made.

HAUSSMANN:

> I hear a voice, but I am not afraid.
> Rather I feel immortal energy
> Flowing from tops of buildings into me!
> And how strange that all along
> I have heard that same strange song:
> "Haussmann, genius, take from me
> Such immortal energy"!

What was this inspiration of my hours?
Oh, are we but the pawns of greater powers?

EDOUARD:

And listen, Haussmann!
Mexico City, Stockholm, Chicago,
Madrid, Philadelphia, Barcelona,
Or, more specifically, Paseo de la Reforma
In Mexico City, and in Chicago
Michigan Boulevard and the lake front,
And in Philadelphia
The Benjamin Franklin Parkway, in Cleveland the
 Mall,
Prefect, your genius will inspire them all!

HAUSSMANN:

Can it be true?

EDOUARD:

Cities, appear!

       (*Enter* CITIES *and* CITIZENS.)

ALL CITIES AND CITIZENS:

We the cities of the future
Sing in gratitude to you!

MAN:

I am an industrial of Chicago.
My business was not going very fine,
Until they built the Lake Shore Drive!
Oh, Haussmann, dear, you are a friend of mine!

COUPLE:

We are young and Cleveland lovers

Who had no place to go at all,
But now we spend our days together
Walking up and down the Cleveland Mall!

SECOND MAN:

I am an adept of Philadelphia
But we had fewer big streets than them all!
Oh now we have the Benjamin Franklin Parkway—
It makes me so excited I could bawl!

ALL THE AMERICANS:

Hail to you, Haussmann!
We poor Americans
Doomed to live in cities that are purely for utility
Owe a debt of gratitude
To your lovely attitude
That great big airy streets and monuments bring life
    facility.
Hail to you, Haussmann—
You've made our evening walks,
Morning strolls, and noontime talks a joy!
We much regret your fall,
Hope that you aren't hurt at all,
And that you will join us—boy oh boy!
Gosh, golly, gee, hooray!
Some evening for a walk upon the Mall!

HAUSSMANN:

Thank you, America. You make my heart beat fast.
Though Paris were torn down, my work should last
In other cities!

EDOUARD:

                                        Paris shall not be

Destroyed until the Beast comes to the Sea.
Let other towns appear!

ROME:

Mi chiamano Roma.
Il Corso io devo a te,
E'i gran prospetti
Fin' a l'eternità!

STOCKHOLM:

Jag talar endast svenska.
Stockholm sono. Swede I am,
The "Venice of the North," but modeled most
On what you've done right here
In Paris!

ALL CITIES:

Oh, Paree!
Every city of the world aspires to be
Like Paree!

MEXICAN MAN:

And I, in Mexico City, spend my days
Admiring the Paseo de la Reforma
And to the mighty Haussmann here give praise!
Olé!

BARCELONA:

I, Barcelona, add the word "Olé!"

ALL CITIES AND CITIZENS:

Olé! Olé!
For Haussmann, who has made a holiday
Of streets and parks that last us through the year

Where there before was naught, was naught
But weekday workday streets all drab and drear!
Olé! Olé!
For the city as a holiday
Of fresh spring air and prospects bright and clear!

EDOUARD:

Cities, disperse! Haussmann, you see
What your future fame shall be.

(CITIES *and* CITIZENS *leave.*)

For helping me, this is your prize:
To live forever in men's eyes!
You have brought Beauty back to me and Paris!

HAUSSMANN:

Oh, our accomplishments shall never know an ending!
What do I care that they criticized my spending?
This vision of the future by this chorus
Makes me aware that the whole world is for us,
And, though my day is over, think of all
The avenues that beauty will cut through—
Think of the grandiose, divine
Designs like mine,
All spacious, grand, and new,
So grand and new!

EDOUARD:

Farewell, thou princely Prefect, oh farewell!
You fell from power—yet, famous ere you fell,
Your fame shall last forever!

HAUSSMANN:
Oh, farewell!

(HAUSSMANN *leaves.*)

ANGELICA:

    Oh, due to you all Paris arrayed
    In housefronts and fresh air—an inspiration
    To all the other cities in the world!
    I love the Avenue Marceau—

EDOUARD:

    And you will love the Ligne de Sceaux
    When it goes underground!
    For Paris has not ceased to change:
    A railroad underground seems strange,
    But it shall come to pass—
    And still the Seine shall shine as bright as glass!
    An Eiffel Tower shall ascend
    Above the Champ de Mars,
    And Frenchmen visiting a love or friend
    Will move about these streets in little cars;
    A Statue of Liberty will be placed
    By the Allée des Cygnes, which does not exist,
    But some morning waking, an early walk taking,
    You'll notice it there in the mist, in the mist, in the
        beautiful bright Paris mist!
    And Haussmann's widened Elysées
    Now so elegant and gray
    Shall on some not-too-distant night
    Be whitened with soft cinematic light!
    Oh, Paris owes
    Its look of a dew-wet, fresh, well-lighted rose,
    Angelica, to your uncertainty.
    Haussmann built it all
    To bring you back to me!

(*They embrace.*)

JEAN (*offstage, from a distance*):
   Angelica. . . . !

PRODUCTION NOTES

Bertha was first produced at The Living Theatre, New York, on December 28, 1959. Directed by Nicola Cerno-vich, with sets and costumes by Remy Charlip, music for solo trumpet by Virgil Thomson, and starring Sudie Bond. In February, 1962, a second production was given at the Cherry Lane Theatre, New York.

Pericles was first produced at the Cherry Lane Theatre, New York, on December 5, 1960. Directed by Nicola Cernovich, with sets and costumes by Robert Mitchell, music by Albert Fine, and with Athan Karras and Nicholas Crabbe in the roles of Pericles and his Friend.

George Washington Crossing the Delaware was first produced at the Maidman Playhouse, New York, in March, 1962. Directed by Arthur Storch, décor and costumes by Alex Katz, and with Richard Libertini and MacIntyre Dixon as Washington and Cornwallis.

The Construction of Boston was first produced at the Maidman Playhouse, New York, on May 4, 1962. This collaboration with Niki de Saint-Phalle, Jean Tinguely, and Robert Rauschenberg was directed by Merce Cunningham; the music was by John Dooley; the Chorus was played by Richard Libertini and MacIntyre Dixon.

Guinevere, or The Death of the Kangaroo was first produced by the American Theatre for Poets in New York in May, 1964. Directed by John Herbert McDowell, sets and costumes by Red Grooms, music by John Herbert McDowell, and with Susan Kaufman as Guinevere.